Think of Me Kindly

Think of Me Kindly

Thoughts on
friendship, nature, love and creativity
from the letters of Ludwig van Beethoven

Edited by Susan Polis Schutz
in conjunction with
SandPiper Studios, Inc.

Illustrated by Stephen Schutz

Blue Mountain Press ™

Boulder, Colorado

Library of Congress Number: 78-59096
ISBN: 0-88396-031-1

Manufactured in the United States of America
First Printing: August, 1978

Acknowledgments:
Quotations selected and edited for inclusion in this book are
standard English translations adapted from the letters of Ludwig
van Beethoven. Recognition is made to the original publishers whose
translations are now in the public domain.

BEETHOVEN: THE MAN AND THE ARTIST, compiled and annotated by
Friedrich Kerst. B. W. Huebsch, Publishers, 1905.

BEETHOVEN'S LETTERS, translated by Lady Wallace. Oliver Ditson
Company, New York, 1866. From the collection of Dr. Ludwig Nohl.

Additional translations by SandPiper Studios, Inc.

Blue Mountain Press INC.

P.O. Box 4549, Boulder, Colorado 80306

CONTENTS

Wherever I am,
you are there
also.

We shall soon surely
see each other . . .
my heart is
overflowing with all I have
to say to you.

I wish you
all possible good
and happiness.

Your letter
made me feel
very happy;
though I do not
frequently write to you,
and you never see me,
still I write you letters
by thousands
in my thoughts.

Slight misunderstandings
sometimes occur between us,
and yet they only serve
to strengthen our friendship.

Friends are not only together
when they are side-by-side,
even one who is far away. . .
is still in our thoughts.

Be calm, for only by calm contemplation of our existence can we attain our aim to live together. Continue to love me . . . Yesterday, today, what longings for you; what tears for you . . . you, my life. Love me forever, and never doubt the faithful heart of your lover.
Ever thine.
Ever mine.
Ever each other's.

Forgive me, my friend,
if I did hurt your feelings;
I was not less a sufferer myself
through not having you near me
during such a long time.
Only then did I really feel
how dear to my heart you are
and ever will be.

Truth exists for the wise;
beauty for the susceptible heart.
They belong together
as complements.

Every day is lost in which
we do not learn something useful.
Man has no nobler or more valuable
possession than time.

Foreign countries will make you gentler, more human, more reconciled to the world.

Every day there are new inquiries from foreigners, new acquaintances, new relationships, even with regard to art. Sometimes my undeserved fame is enough to drive me mad; fortune is seeking me out, and this almost makes me fear some new misfortune.

If I told you that the verses you just sent me did not perplex me, I should tell a lie. It is a peculiar sensation to see, to hear one's self praised, and then to be conscious of one's weakness, as I am. I always look upon such opportunities as warnings to approach nearer, however difficult it may be, to the unattainable goal which art and nature set before us.

Oh! Gaze at nature in all its beauty, and calmly accept the inevitable — love demands everything, and rightly so. Thus it is for me with thee, as for thee with me.

I wish to you
all earthly happiness
with your souls united,
in thought
I kiss and embrace
all your dear children,
and wish
that you may know this;
but I commend myself to you,
and only add,
that I shall never forget
and always willingly recall,
the hours which I have spent
in company with you.

I rejoice at
the mere thought
of seeing you.

The bond of friendship and soul unites us. I loudly proclaim myself, now as ever, Your loving friend and admirer.

Advise your critics to exercise more care and good sense with regard to the productions of young authors; for many a one of them may lose their creative spirit, who otherwise might have risen to higher things. For myself, though I am indeed far from considering myself to have attained such a degree of perfection as to be beyond censure, the outcry at first of your critics against me was too humiliating.

I never answer insults.
Anything else, "how" or "why"
I have done something,
I am ready to explain at any minute.

My prayer
is that you may enjoy
a happier life,
and one more free from care,
than mine has been.
Recommend to your children Virtue;
it alone can bring happiness,
and not wealth.
I speak from experience.
It was Virtue which sustained me
in times of trouble.
To her, and to my Art,
I owe thanks.

I have continually hoped that my presence might give you rest and serenity, and that you would reveal yourself trustful of me. I hope for a better tomorrow, and pray that there will still be a few hours for us to spend and to enjoy together amid the beauties of nature.

Even before I rise, my thoughts go out to you, my beloved - sometimes full of joy, and then again with sorrow, waiting to see whether fate will take pity on us. Either I must live wholly with you or not at all. I have resolved to wander in distant lands, until I can fly to your arms, and feel that with you, I have a real home.

I know of no more sacred duty than to rear and educate a child.

I am once again leading a more pleasant life, for I have been associating with other people . . . This change has been brought about by an enchanting maiden, who loves me, and whom I love. Once again after two years, I have had some blissful moments, and for the first time I feel that marriage can bring happiness.

My ears are buzzing and ringing perpetually, day and night. I can with truth say that my life is very wretched; for nearly two years past I have avoided all society, because I find it impossible to say to people, "I am deaf!"

In any other profession this might be more tolerable, but in mine such a condition is truly frightful . . .

Some time ago, quiet, peaceful life came to an end for me. I have been forcibly drawn into public life; as yet I have attained no good result from this, perhaps the reverse — but who has not been affected by the storms around us?

Still, I should not only be happy, but the happiest of men, if a demon had not taken up his abode in my ears.

I have just spent the last six months in the country . . . how humiliating it was, when someone standing close to me heard a flute in the far distance, while I heard nothing. Or when others heard a shepherd singing, and again I heard nothing. Such incidents almost drove me to despair; at times I was on the verge of putting an end to my life. Art — art alone restrained my hand! Oh, it seemed as if I could not quit this earth until I had produced all I felt within me.

Although I have suffered much, I have not yet lost my innermost feelings for childhood, for exquisite nature or for friendship.

Try and manage for us to come together and remain together — on my side, I will certainly do my best. You will always find me frank, without any reserve in this relationship. In short, everything I do may show you how willingly I enter into an association with you.

I wish you all that is good and beautiful in life.
Keep me, and willingly, in remembrance (forgiving my wild behavior).
Be convinced that no one more than myself can desire to know that your life is joyous and prosperous.
I am your most devoted servant and friend.

How earnestly shall I strive
to pass my life with you,
and what a life it shall be!
. . . However dearly you may love me,
I love you more fondly still.
Never conceal your feelings from me
. . . for our love is truly a celestial mansion,
as firm as heaven itself.

My favorite realm
is that of the mind and the spirit.
I regard it as the highest of all
worldly and spiritual monarchies.
Do let me know what you want of me,
of my poor musical faculties,
so that I may create something for your
own musical sense of feelings,
as far as I am able to comply.

Even though wild surges often accuse my heart, it still is good. To do good wherever we can, to love liberty above all things, and never to deny truth though it be at the throne itself . . . these things I believe.

I used to be too free with my judgments and made enemies in this way; now I judge no one, and for no other reason than that I want to harm no one, and in the end I say to myself; if there's something decent in anyone, it will be upheld.

I must recuperate
amid unspoilt nature
and cleanse my mind.
Would you like
to come with me today
to visit my unalterable friends,
the green shrubs and the aspiring trees,
the green hedges and bowers
with their murmuring streams?
Here there is no envy
or competition
or dishonesty.
Do come . . .
what a glorious morning!
It promises a fine day.

Almighty in the forest.
I am happy, blissful
in the forest.
Every tree speaks through you.
Oh, God, what splendor!
In such a wooded scene,
on the heights
there is such a calm.

Surrounded by nature's beauty,
often I sit for hours,
while my senses feast
upon the spectacles of nature.
Here the majestic sun is not concealed
. . . here the blue sky
is my sublime roof.
When in the evening
I contemplate the sky in wonder
and the host of luminous bodies
continually revolving within their orbits,
suns or earths by name,
then my spirit rises
beyond these constellations
so many millions of miles away.

I am as happy as a child
at the thought of wandering
among clusters of bushes,
in the woods, among trees, herbs, rocks . . .
No man loves the countryside
more than I. For do not forests, trees, and rocks
re-echo that for which mankind longs?

If ever you go to the old towns and
ruins, think to yourself that Beethoven
lingered there. If you should wander
through the enchanted pine forests,
think that it was there Beethoven
so often composed.

Never shall I forget
the days which I spent with you . . .
Continue to be my friend,
as you will always find me yours.

I will vouch for it
that the pure temple
of holy friendship
which you will erect
will for ever stand firm;
no chance event,
no storm
will be able to
shake its foundations
- firm -
- eternal -
our friendship.

I am very free in speech.
I am perfectly natural
with all my friends,
and hate all restraint . . .
If anything I do
displeases them,
friendship demands
only for them to tell me so,
and I will certainly
take care not to offend again . . .
Misunderstanding and resolve
. . . will only serve to render our
friendship ever more firm.

You will ask me where I get my ideas. That I cannot tell you with certainty; they come unsummoned, directly, indirectly — I could seize them with my hands — out in the open air; in the woods, while walking; in the silence of the nights; early in the morning; incited by moods, which are translated by the poet into words, by me into tones that sound, and roar and storm about me until I have set them down in notes.

I carry my thoughts about with me for a long time, often a very long time, before I write them down. Meanwhile, my memory is so faithful that I am sure never to forget, not even in years, a theme that has once occurred to me. I change many things, discard, and try again until I am satisfied. Then, however, there begins in my head the development in every direction; and, inasmuch as I know exactly what I want, the fundamental idea never deserts me. It arises before me, grows, and I see and hear the picture in all its extent and dimensions stand before my mind like a cast. There remains for me nothing but the labor of writing it down, which is quickly accomplished when I have the time.

A musician is also a poet, and the magic of a pair of eyes can suddenly cause him to feel transported into a more beautiful world . . . I cannot tell what ideas came into my head when I made your acquaintance . . . that was a precious moment for me. The most beautiful melodies glided from your eyes into my heart, which one day will enchant the world . . . long after Beethoven has ceased to conduct.

I have never thought of writing merely for reputation and honor. What I have in my heart and soul — must find a way out. That is the reason why I compose.

For me there is no pleasure so great as to promote and pursue my art.

The true artist is not proud, he unfortunately sees that art has no limits; he feels darkly how far he is from the goal. And though he may be admired by others, he is often sad not to have reached that point to which his better genius only appears as a distant, guiding sun.

There ought to be only one grand artistic depot where the artist need only hand in his artwork in order to receive what he asks for. As things stand now, one must be half a business man, and how is this to be endured? Good heavens! that is what I really call "troublesome."

If you feel as though it would be convenient to pay me a visit, I should be delighted. But if you find it unbecoming, you know how I honor the freedom of all men. However you may act in this or in any other case, according to your principles and your caprice, you will always find in me the acceptance of a friend.

May heaven have
you and yours
in its keeping . . .
I hope that we
shall often have
opportunity to
assure ourselves
that you are a
great friend to me,
and that I am
your devoted
brother and friend.

The good and beautiful
needs no assistance.
It exists
without outward help,
and this seems
to be the reason
for our enduring
friendship.

Oh! life is so beautiful,
it would be glorious to live
one's life a thousand
times over.

I kiss you
on your forehead,
imprinting on it,
as with a seal,
all my thoughts for you.

Always remain a faithful, good, honest friend. That I could ever forget you, and especially all of you who were so kind and affectionate to me, no, do not believe it; there are moments in which I myself long for you — yes, and wish to spend some time with you. — My native land, the beautiful country in which I first saw the light of the world, is ever as beautiful and distinct before mine eyes as when I left you. In short, I shall regard that time as one of the happiest of my life, when I see you again.

Today happens to be Sunday,
and I shall read you something
out of the Gospels:
"Love one another."

The only good thing
is a beautiful, benevolent soul,
which is revealed in everything,
and from which nothing needs to hide.

I am careless in replying to my friends, because I believe those whom I really love know me without my writing to them. I often get an answer ready in my thoughts; but, when I want to put it on paper, I mostly throw away my pen, because I cannot write as I feel. I do remember every kindness you have shown me.

Think sometimes of one
who always thinks of you.

I wish you all the good and charm
that life can offer. Think of me kindly,
and . . . rest assured that no one
would more rejoice to hear of your
happiness.